Too Hot

by Roger Huth and Alison Hawes
illustrated by Aleksandar Sotirovski

Titles in the Travellers series

Level 3
Goal!	Jane A C West
Too Hot	Roger Hurn/Alison Hawes

Level 4
A Big Catch	Alison Hawes
Deyda's Drum	Roger Hurn
The Strawberry Thief	Alison Hawes
Billy's Boy	Melanie Joyce

Level 5
Cage Boy	Jillian Powell
Master Blasters	Melanie Joyce
Game Player King	Stan Cullimore
In the Zone	Tony Norman

Level 6
Dodgems	Jane A C West
Tansy Smith	Helen Orme

Level 7
Pirate Attack	Jonny Zucker
Hitting the Basket	Jonny Zucker

Badger Publishing Limited
Oldmedow Road, Hardwick Industrial Estate,
King's Lynn PE30 4JJ
Telephone: 01438 791037

www.badgerlearning.co.uk
2 4 6 8 10 9 7 5 3

Too Hot ISBN 978 1 84691 853 7

First edition © 2010
This second edition © 2014

Text © Roger Hurn and Alison Hawes 2010
Complete work © Badger Publishing Limited 2010

Publisher: David Jamieson Editor:
Danny Pearson
Design: Fiona Grant
Illustration: Aleksandar Sotirovski

Too Hot

Contents

Badger
LEARNING

"You are good cooks," says the teacher.
"Will you both cook a dish for our 'Taste the World Day'?"

"A famous chef will taste all the dishes.
He will pick the best one."

TASTE the
WORLD DAY

"I will cook an okra curry," says Rani.

"So will I," says Nita. "But mine will be the best."

Rani cooks an okra curry at home.

She tries it out on her family.

"Do you like it?" she asks.

"It is great," they say.

"It is not too hot. It is just right. Your dish will be the best!"

Rani frowns. "But what if the chef hates curry?"

"He will love it," they say. "Just don't make it too hot!"

It is 'Taste the World Day' at Rani's school.

The children cook their dishes.

All the food looks very tasty.
But Nita is angry.

Rani's curry is better than hers.
So Nita tips extra chilli onto it!

Rani is very upset.
Her curry is too hot now.

The famous chef tries all the dishes.
Then he tries Rani's okra curry.

He makes a face. Is it too hot?

Nita grins.

Rani looks sad.

Then the chef smiles.

"I love very hot curry," he says.
"This is the best dish!"

Questions

Who asks Rani and Nita to cook at the 'Taste the World Day'?

Who will be at the 'Taste the World Day'?

Who wins 'Taste the World Day'?

Story 2
Nadya's Photos

Main characters:

Nadya

Mark

Kate

Vocabulary

Photo	Camera
Snatches	Friend
New	Country

Nadya says goodbye to her
old school.

She takes a photo of her friends.

Nadya says goodbye to her old country.

She takes a photo of her family.

Nadya takes her photos to her new country.

She takes the photos to her new school.
Mark takes Nadya's photos.

Mark snatches the camera out of her hand.

He runs off.

But Kate takes them back!

Nadya shows Kate her photos.

She shows Kate her friends and family.

Kate shows Nadya round her new town.

Nadya shows Kate a photo of her new friend.

It is a photo of Kate!

Questions

Who does Nadya take photos of before she leaves her old country?

Who takes Nadya's photos and camera from her?

Who is Nadya's new friend?

Story 3
Something from Nothing

Main characters

Fahim

Babor

Mum

Vocabulary

Alive   Camp
Belongings   Tent
Nothing   Something

They are alive.

But they have no money and no belongings.

They have nothing.

Fahim, Babor and their mum walk for days.

They have no food and no water.

They have nothing.

They come to a camp.

Fahim, Babor and their mum have a tent.

They have food and water and...

...they have each other.

They have something.

One day they will be able to go home.

Questions

Where are Fahim, Babor and their mum walking to?

How long do they walk for?

What do they get at the camp?